THE BIBLICAL IMAGE

OF THE FAMILY

THE
BIBLICAL
Image
OF THE
FAMILY

WEBB GARRISON

TIDINGS, NASHVILLE, TENNESSEE

THE BIBLICAL IMAGE OF THE FAMILY

Copyright © 1965
TIDINGS
1908 Grand Avenue
Nashville, Tennessee

*Library of Congress Catalog
Card Number: 65-17327*

The cover emblem symbolizes man and wife united in holy matrimony. The two linked circles are like wedding rings, ancient symbols of human love. But the circle is also a symbol of God's perfect plan. It is His will that man and woman be united in Christ and that they have the same relation as Christ and his Church.

P

PRINTED IN THE UNITED STATES OF AMERICA

Introduction

IN this volume Webb Garrison has provided the Church with a scriptural study book examining the basic structure of the family in the light of both Old and New Testament insights and counsel. Discussing the role and position of the family as they apply to marriage, the father, the mother, the children, divorce, and adultery, Dr. Garrison emphasizes family enrichment through the use of the Bible and the practice of Christian family living in the community.

The present volume thus seeks to examine the contemporary family in the light of biblical standards for the purpose of establishing spiritual guidelines to creative family living. The insights which the author presents here constitute the kind of scriptural exploration which makes for a deeper understanding of the quality of true faith. Where families study these insights together, they will discover the hope which rests in a genuine commitment to the ideals of Jesus Christ.

THE EDITORS

Contents

Contents

Chapter 1
Marriage

AT 8:35 A.M., students were still filing into the New York Avenue public school, Indianapolis. Though patrol boys gestured for her to hurry, a girl of eight or nine paid them no attention.

Yellow pigtails bobbing as she flashed the whole world a snaggle-toothed smile, the girl held a few blossoms of lily-of-the-valley, their stalks wrapped in aluminum foil. With the bouquet precisely at her waistline, she walked stiff-legged and chanted the wedding march at the top of her voice.

For her that day, a forthcoming wedding was more important than school, teachers, patrol boys, passing motorists, her lessons, and whether or not the sun was shining.

In a strange and special sense, the Bible is as preoccupied with marriage as was that school girl. For in Scripture, the union of man and wife is the most important of all human relationships. That being the case, it is not strange, but inevitable that marriage enters deeply into the basic symbolism which seeks to describe the divine-human encounter.

On the human level, mutual self-yielding of two partners is the central aspect of marriage. " 'God made them male and female.' 'For this reason a man shall leave his father and mother and be joined to his wife, and the two shall become one.' So they are no longer two but one" (Mark 10:6-8).

Surrender—or lowering the protective walls that surround the ego—is the most difficult and also the most enriching aspect of marriage. It is the key to an enduring union; for when persons so guard their private selves that they remain two instead of one, separation or divorce may result. Surrender is the key to enlargement of self; when walls tumble down, each self so flows into the other that both are enlarged in achieving a new unity.

This means that genuine marriage is a paradoxical blending of giving-in-receiving. It involves a once-for-all, unbreakable, irreversible decision. In marriage, the wife literally no longer belongs to herself but to her husband—and the husband literally belongs to his wife rather than himself. Even Paul, whose views of marriage are rather special, concedes that "the wife does not rule over her own body, but the husband does; likewise the husband does not rule over his own body, but the wife does" (1 Cor. 7:4).

Self-identity is preserved and individuality is enhanced instead of diminished in marriage. Still there must be the powerful growth-process of giving without reserve. So long as there are restrictions and conditions and reservations and stipulations and conditional clauses, a marriage may be perfectly legal and respectable and may endure for seventy-five years—but it is less than full, mature, adequate.

Part of the difficulty and much of the glory of marriage lies in the fact that the partner who now "has power over the other" is a changing individual whose demands vary from one day and one year to the next. There is no once-for-all achievement of full and total solutions, no unchangeable achievement of satisfactory personal change. Here is a dynamic process of growth at its most sublime level.

No wonder, therefore, that in his *Philosophy of Religion* Elton Trueblood draws comparisons between marriage and religious commitment. Both, he points out, require an unconditional agreement. Each sets up a situation in which there is no turning back, no matter what may come. It is for this reason, he insists, that the metaphor of marriage has been so widely used to throw light on the relation between the divine and the human.

Old Testament Use of the Marriage Metaphor

At least as early as the Eighth Century, B.C., the relationship between Jehovah and His Chosen People was expressed by the great prophets in terms of marriage. Isaiah comforts Israel by singing:

> Your Maker is your husband.
> . . . .
> For the Lord has called you
>   like a wife forsaken and grieved in spirit,
> like a wife of youth when she is cast off (Isaiah 54:5-6).

Hosea glories in the fact that God will not divorce Israel even for her unfaithfulness. Jeremiah contrasts woes and calamities with joy and merriment of the divine-human wedding feast. Isaiah stresses the promise that God's desolate people will be given a new name, Beulah (Hebrew for "married"). When this takes place, he promises, God will rejoice over Israel as the bridegroom rejoices over the bride. (See Isaiah 62:4-5).

These references, and many others like them, stress the fact that marriage is the most sublime union into which man and woman may enter as partners.

Indeed, in the Genesis story of the creation of the world and its inhabitants, there is a clear but often overlooked emphasis according to which marriage is essential to being fully human! "God created man in his own image, in the image of God he created him; male and female he created them" (Genesis 1:27). It takes both male and female to form the genus, "man." Separately, neither is a whole human being; it is only when man and woman are united that true "man" emerges—made in the image of God.

As with individual men and women on the human plane, so with mankind as a whole in relation to God. It is only when Israel becomes the Bride of Jehovah that she begins fully to exhibit the reasons for her existence. In her exalted role, Israel often wavers and sometimes wanders from the path of virtue. But her divine Lover never wavers. Often pleading, frequently paying court, and sometimes threatening dire vengeance, Jehovah clings to Israel His Bride in a fashion that logic can never explain.

This is the one fundamental and overwhelming note of the entire Old Testament. For reasons that even the Chosen People did not pretend to understand, the Creator of the heavens and the earth chose an obscure group of tribesmen as His own. It was out of His "marriage" with Israel that a Son was born in the fullness of time—one whom men called Immanuel, who came in order to offer all men the Good News of rescue through him.

New Testament Use of the Marriage Metaphor

In John's Gospel, the first miracle of which we have an account is linked with a wedding feast at Cana in Galilee. Perhaps you remember the strange doings there: Water is turned into wine, in a situation where everyone from Mary the mother of Jesus to the master of the wedding feast seems strangely bewildered by events. (See John 2:1-11.)

For the Gospel writer, this story is a vehicle to communicate the utterly incredible and astonishing message: Jesus of Nazareth, the heavenly Bridegroom, has come to claim the Church as his Bride!

"I feel a divine jealousy for you," Paul confesses to members of the congregation in Corinth, "for I betrothed you to Christ to present you as a pure bride to her one husband" (2 Cor. 11:2). In precisely the same spirit, John of Patmos regards the whole Christian fellowship as "the Bride, the wife of the Lamb" (Rev. 21:9).

Two-Way Flow of Ideas

This hasty survey makes it quite clear that, in the Biblical image of the family, human marriage has influenced religious symbolism—and that deep-rooted spiritual forces operated to give the Chosen People a high and idealistic concept of marriage.

In the life of a man and woman living in the space age, precisely the same-two-way flow of ideas can be operative.

More than any other human relationship, marriage can throw light upon the personal transformation that takes place when a person "surrenders to Jesus Christ"—or enters a marriage contract with the Saviour.

By the same token, a vigorous spiritual life rooted in the Bible and watered by participation in the corporate life of the Church is the most vital single factor contributing to a good and lasting marriage.

FOR DISCUSSION

Marriage is often difficult and demanding. If God had cared to do so, doubtless He could have created a world in which marriage and sexual union would not be necessary for reproduction. Why do you suppose He created us so that, individually, each of us is incomplete and "unfinished"?

Many persons who have been in Sunday school and church all their lives know a few New Testament passages that refer to marriage but have never given any thought to symbolic references. In view of the fact that the marriage metaphor runs through the entire Bible, do you have any theory to account for this neglect of it?

Roman Catholic interpreters regard the Song of Songs (or Song of Solomon) as filled with basic Christian messages. Many of their Bible students, who refer to this ancient poem as Canticles, rank it along with the Psalms and major prophetic books as among the most important literature of Old Testament times. Many Protestant scholars consider it a pagan love song that got into the Bible only because Solomon's name was attached to it. Read this brief book, one of the most neglected in the Bible, and discuss the evidence for and against the view that it is a great spiritual classic.

Chapter 2

The Family

PLAINFIELD, Indiana, has several unusual street names. A traveller passing through town from east to west on U.S. Highway 40 will notice the queerest of them all at the west edge of the community. For there an ordinary-looking street bears the name: "Wedding Lane."

What an address! Think of it—for years to have your mail directed to "Wedding Lane"!

Weddings are wonderful. But a wedding atmosphere is not one in which to live for life. There must be a moving past the climactic, emotion-packed hour. There must be a maturing, a growing together on the part of the man and woman who now may be mother and father instead of bride and groom.

In surveying some ideas about marriage and some uses of the marriage metaphor, we have just crossed the threshold in our look at "The Biblical Image of the Family." Moving forward, we shall very quickly discover that, in some respects, the Scriptural view of the family is strange and alien to us.

A Community Formed by Kinship

Especially in Old Testament times, the Hebrew family was big and comprehensive. Headed by the oldest male, the group included not only sons and daughters, brothers and sisters (until their marriage), grandsons and granddaughters, but also nieces and nephews, cousins and half-brothers.

Perhaps you have noticed in your reading of the Old Testament that many of the early leaders (Abraham, for example) circumcised all the males in the household. Slaves, foreigners, and even hired servants were included in this rite, so vital in the religious and social life of Israel.

Circumcision was a *religious*, not a medical, ceremony. It involved, of course, the male organ of generation. Consequently it "proclaimed" that the man who had undergone this holy rite was dedicated to Jehovah—and Him alone—in and through his sexual organ. Circumcision led to "kinship in Jehovah," with the result that a slave or a foreigner who received the rite became just as much a part of the family as those who were bound to it by bonds of blood.

Viewed in this comprehensive sense, the family was the unit of all activity. Whenever a census was taken, it was made along family lines. Great care was taken to preserve genealogical records because a man's place in the larger community might be determined by his ancestry. Long before writing became common, it was standard practice to memorize elaborate lists that traced one's family for generations.

It is this fundamental importance of the family that accounts for the presence of so many genealogical lists in Scripture. Dull as they may be to us, they were of urgent importance at the time they were committed to writing.

There is no infancy narrative in the fourth Gospel because the apostle John is preoccupied with the transcendent Saviour who helped to create the world. But both Matthew and Luke find it necessary to trace Jesus' ancestry. For Matthew, Jesus Christ could not be who he is, were he not "the son of David, the son of Abraham" (Matt. 1:1). In spite of his emphasis upon the fact that Joseph was not the father of Jesus, Luke traces the ancestry of his Lord through Joseph, all the way back to Adam, the original "son of God" (Luke 3:23-38).

All persons within a family, no matter how many generations were involved, are considered literally to be *one flesh*. Thus the family extends both forward and backward in time. All who belong to it, either by birth, adoption, or circumcision, are part and parcel of one another. No other claim can take precedence over the claim of the family; no other ties are so binding.

Family Rules Govern Marriage

Quite early, there was a distinction between betrothal—roughly equivalent to modern engagement—and marriage itself. Agreements were made, not by the persons anticipating marriage, but by the heads of their respective families. There was no preliminary courtship, no insistence upon the necessity of falling in love. Indeed, there was a much-quoted proverb to the effect that "love comes after marriage, not before."

It was taken for granted that everyone capable of it would enter into marriage. Among the early Hebrews, there were widows but no spinsters. Especially in time of war, the number of women was likely to exceed the number of men. This was a basic factor in the practice of polygamy, which has puzzled many readers of the Bible. With every woman expected to marry and bear children even during times when there was a scarcity of husband material, multiple marriage was the natural, if not the inevitable answer.

In practically every case, a father who arranged the marriage of his daughter was expected to make a payment to the family into which she entered. This meant that there was a contract, or covenant, between the families as well as the marriage partners.

The Family as a Religious Community

Training of children was largely in the hands of the family during the entire period in which the Bible was formed, though there were some synagogue schools in New Testament times. The family served as glue to hold society together. Through the family, members of "younger generations" learned the traditions of the past and the customs of worship.

It is the religious character of the family group that accounts for the central significance of circumcision. By that act, a man child born into the family was united with the family's God—and through it a foreigner or stranger could simultaneously become a follower of Jehovah and a member of the family.

Strange as some of these ancient practices sound to us today, we cannot escape realizing that, to an extent quite without parallel in history, the Jews have preserved their beliefs and their way of life. "Juvenile delinquency" is virtually unknown among modern American Jews, for the bonds of the family are still so tight that boys and girls are not turned loose to wander the streets and follow their own inclinations. At this point, Christians could well learn a great deal from their Jewish neighbors.

Yet the Church itself might not have come into existence had not early Christians made their families function as religious communities. There is little doubt that the earliest churches were "house churches"—little bands of believers in Jesus Chirst for whom a family served as a nucleus and who came into homes in order to pray, read Scripture, sing, and observe the holy feast of the Lord's Supper. Children reared in such an environment were giuded and shaped in a fashion utterly impossible to us who go to a special building for our worship and send our children to spend half their time in schoolrooms far removed from the family's influence.

The author of the Letter to the Hebrews urges us that we must "exhort one another every day, as long as it is called 'today,' that none of you may be hardened by the deceitfulness of sin" (Hebrews 3:13). Such exhortation is a rather spontaneous process taking place within a we-group. It involves a state of mutual tolerance, of which the best example is the atmosphere within a happy family. Though all members preserve their individuality and actually have it enhanced by the process, each in the group is free to speak frankly—even critically on occasion—but always in the atmosphere of knowing that each loves the other and will sacrifice for the other.

So viewed, the family as a religious community is the highest and most holy expression of "group dynamics." Every person needs the sometimes gentle and sometimes stinging exhortation of others with whom he is in a state of mutual love and tolerance. To be shielded or protected from that kind of exhortation is to form a crust that inhibits the growth of the self. It is a hardening of the secretions of the ego, so that this very fearful form of sin encrusts the shielded personality. Hence the family in which "daily exhortation" proceeds spontaneously in love is the most growth-inducing climate man can experience.

A Climate for Growth—Ordained by God

Since the Biblical image of the family is first spiritual and then physical or material, it follows that devotion to God is the first consideration of mother and father, son and daughter. Instead of being a human arrangement upon which men stumbled, the family is an instrument of the divine purpose. It is one of the tools—and among the most vital of them all—used by God the Creator in his continuous work of shaping the world and mankind.

So viewed, marriage is not simply a contract made in keeping with prevailing laws and subject to dissolution under their terms. Instead, it is, in the words of *The Interpreter's Dictionary of the Bible,* "a personal-sexual spiritual companionship ordained and instituted by God."

For Discussion

It is abundantly clear that many forces in modern American life run completely counter to preservation of the family in the Biblical sense. Do you think we may as well surrender to attacking forces and give up the attempt to have families that are "religious communities," or are there specific things that can be done to strengthen and restore such a view of the family?

Discuss the implications of the following advertisement:—

Dear Friendly Food Lover. . . . You deserve to eat out often!
Togetherness—the whole family eats out in a happy, friendly mood—always more tender, pleasant words are spoken in public dining. The

little ones sense this, and take on the responsibility of behaving when away from home. Thus providing a good atmosphere for cultured growth—education in meeting people. Also helps mother mend frayed nerves from housewifeitis.

HAVE DAD EAT OUT WITH SON OR DAUGHTER—just by themselves. This will give busy Dad a better opportunity to get acquainted with his child. Today's very strenuous economic pressures on "dear old dad" are far too demanding, leaving only a small bit of time for his children. There is something thrilling, exciting, the way the young will open up, warm up, and understand father's many "headachey" problems when eating together at this restaurant.

To inspire togetherness, we present 6 coupons for family dining: Togetherness, Dad and Son, Dad and Daughter. Yours for friendly dining. . . .

Chapter 3

Father and Husband

IT IS literally impossible to over-emphasize the significance of father-hood in Scripture. There are many dimensions to the father-idea, of course. Some of them are human, while others involve the divine-human relationship. But measured by the single standard of the number of references, fatherhood emerges as one of the central emphases of the entire Bible.

In the famous volume, *An Exhaustive Concordance of the Bible*, by James Strong, the words "family" and "families" occupy just a bit more than two columns. But nearly nine columns are required to list the points at which "father" occurs in Scripture, while the plural form "fathers" occupies another five columns.

The importance of the father/husband is just as great in the realm of ideas as in terms of space occupied. Indeed, to revise the concept of the father of the household and the Father of all mankind as depicted in the Bible is to alter the whole Biblical picture of human life and its meaning. Whether we have intended to do so or not, in the modern church we have in practice made

20

radical changes in our concept of the father's role. The nature and extent of such changes are best recognized by a quick survey of the Biblical concept of the father's authority and responsibility.

Authority and Responsibility of the Father

Within the family, the father had supreme authority. Since this authority attached to the most powerful (often, but not always the oldest) male in the clan, the "father" was often a grandfather or even a great-grandfather.

He stood for the solidarity of the family and symbolized both its demonstrated power of survival from the past and its hope of "many children" in the future. In a sense that we moderns find both strange and very difficult to grasp, the significance of a family was largely determined by the father. No matter how many fighting men might be numbered in its ranks or how many cattle and sheep were owned, a family headed by a weak or corrupt father was regarded as inferior. But a strong, wise, and good father sheltered every member of his family under the umbrella of his own strength and prestige.

For the individual in Old Testament times, the very meaning of his life comes to focus in the person and nature of his father. As "possessor and master" of the family, the father has many qualities we today associate with a ruler. But the relationship is not at all that of a ruler and his subjects. Rather, it is a great deal more intimate and pervasive. The father is the "center of significance," with capacity to radiate strengtth to the entire circle that is formed about him. All the domestic animals and all the property were under the control of the father.

Obedience to the father was expected as a matter of course. You have to read only a few hours in the Old Testament, however, to discover that sons, daughters, and other members of the family were no nearer perfection then than now. Time after time, a son or a daughter disappoints or defies the father. See, for example, accounts of the behavior of the sons of Noah, the sons of Jacob (brothers of Joseph), and even the sons of the great King David.

Important as it was, the authority of the father was no one-sided concept. Instead, it was matched by a lofty idea of the father's responsibility. He was expected not only to provide for the material needs of his wife and children, but also to set them a high moral example. Though a father had the right to offer up his own sons in sacrifice (Genesis 22), he also had the duty to teach them devotion to Jehovah and fidelity to the inherited traditions of the family. No responsibility of a son ranked above that of hearing, remembering, and putting into practice the unwritten code of his people:

> Hear, my son, your father's instruction,
>   and reject not your mother's teaching;
> for they are a fair garland for your head,
>   and pendants for your neck (Proverbs 1:8-9).

A father's blessing, traditionally conferred upon his oldest son in a special way, was considered a source of special benefit. On the other hand, a father's rebuke constituted a grievous wound to the spirit. It was the oral blessing of blind Isaac over which Jacob and Esau schemed and fought. (See Genesis 27.) Something of the same sense of power was involved in the idea that a father's sins could affect the eternal destiny of his descendants —literally, and not merely figuratively.

All these ideas, summed up, meant that to be a "father" was at once to have the greatest honor that any man could achieve and to receive the most fearful load of responsibility that could be placed upon human shoulders.

Symbolic Use of the Idea of Fatherhood

Years ago in Sunday school, perhaps you wondered why God is always addressed as "Father" and never as "Mother." Children often notice such things as this and ask questions about them; adults who become accustomed to a set of ideas tend to take them for granted and to cease thinking or wondering about them.

Female deities abound in pagan religions. For the highly sophisticated cults of the later Greek cities to the primitive religious practices of peoples untouched by Western influence, it is common to find goddesses of every type and variety. Several major oriental religions include a similar emphasis.

Without qualification or exceptions, Hebrew thought makes God male. And the most common and pervasive of all titles for deity is "Father." Any attempt to give a complete explanation for this unique set of affairs is bound to fail. For this band of people, made up of human families in whose fathers center authority and responsibility, is declared—as an article of faith—to have been chosen by God.

Notice that the Bible does not attempt to explain why God should have made Israel His bride. This is not a relationship to be explained and analyzed—but to be accepted and acted upon.

The use of "Father" as a symbol, to indicate something of the nature of the God who created us and who is so vast our little minds can contain only a fraction of His being, creates a two-way flow of influences. First, it helps us to understand our mighty Creator by applying to Him some of the traits of the ideal father of a family. Second, it challenges every father to live in such fashion that members of his family and others who come in contact with him will be stirred to praise God and not to curse the day they were born or to fall into despair at the future of the human race.

Jesus Christ gave new depth and fresh meaning to the concept of "God the Father." Inevitably, we who have been exposed to the New Testament as well as to the Old Tesament, are profoundly affected by this aspect of the Saviour's message. Especially in the Gospels of Matthew and John, Jesus gives such great emphasis to "Father" that all other titles for deity pale by comparison. More important even than the verbal stress, however, is the way in which Jesus Christ exhibited the power of the Father-Son relationship as the guiding force in life.

Viewed in its total sweep, the Biblical image of the family so stresses the unique and unduplicated role of the father that we find ourselves pausing to ask whether or not all the "progress" we talk about in human relations is genuine or imaginary.

For Discussion

The whole subject of "juvenile delinquency" is a slippery one. In the first place, the term itself is new—it was not used even in the time of our great-grandparents. In the second place, laws are continually in the process of revision. This means that statistics about our "alarming increase in juvenile delinquency" are highly suspect; we don't have a long-range basis for clear comparisons. In spite of this difficulty, do you think the decline of authority and responsibility on the part of the father is a factor in the rising rates of juvenile delinquency?

It would be sheer folly to suggest that modern Americans try to turn back the clock and recapture the family life of ancient Israel. Do you think this fact makes it useless to see what the Bible teaches about the family and its members? If not, what can you do to help your loved ones gain some of the power and solidarity so prominent in the Biblical concept of the family?

Chapter 4

Mother and Wife

OUR hasty survey of the role of the father/husband in Hebrew life and Biblical thought is one-sided and unbalanced without a look at the mother/wife. For the male's authority, though real and decisive, did not lead to the treatment of women as "inferior." On the contrary, a strong argument can be made for the fact that the wife and mother of Bible times actually had a great deal more personal freedom and influence upon the family than the modern working mother who spends little time with her children and is continually harried by demands of simultaneously holding an outside job and keeping house.

That women actually acted boldly and independently even in the very earliest period in the life of the Chosen People can be seen by a quick look at what two of them did.

Rachel, daughter of the wealthy shepherd Laban, is famous as the wife of Jacob and the mother of Joseph. One of the most puzzling and revealing incidents of her career is described, very briefly, in Genesis 31. Jacob, having determined to set off for the homeland of his ancestors, arranged to leave during Laban's absence—taking with him flocks and herbs that belonged to him under his agreement with his father-in-law.

Rachel not only encouraged her husband to decamp; she also stole her father's household gods and took them with her (Genesis 31:19). Generations of Bible scholars have puzzled over this strange act. Recent archaeological discoveries have yielded the first logical explanation for Rachel's conduct. According to secular records from the time and place where these strange events took place, family law of the epoch required property to pass to the male descendants. But there was an exception. If a daughter shared in her father's estate for one reason or another, it was customary for him to hand his household gods over to his daughter's husband.

In the case of Jacob and Rachel, possession of the household gods constituted proof that Jacob was not in illegal possession of animals from the flocks of his father-in-law. That is, Rachel took the law into her own hands and seized for her husband the flocks that he had earned but which her father would not willingly give up! Eclipsed in generations of oral transmission, the story preserved the account of Rachel's bold actions but failed to explain the reasons for them.

An even bolder and more dramatic act by a woman is linked with the little-known wife of Heber the Kenite. After his defeat in battle, the great Canaanite chieftain Sisera—who commanded "nine hundred chariots of iron"—fled on foot. He asked for refuge in the tent of Heber and the shepherd's wife, Jael, made the military chief comfortable. As soon as he was asleep, though, Jael took a tent peg and a hammer and killed the enemy of her people (Judges 4:12-22).

High Status of the Biblical Mother

Scholars think that the Old Testament word for "mother" is adapted from a term meaning "to be wide." Certainly her role in bearing children was a basic one. For centuries, it was considered a source of shame for a woman to be barren. Elizabeth, wife of Zechariah, entered her "old age" deeply grieved that she had not borne a son. But after she did give birth to John, the boy's mother was probably the most important influence upon his character and life. Hence John the Baptist in the New Testament and Samuel in the Old Testament give particularly full and vivid insight into the influence of a devout, strong-willed woman.

Though the father was head of the family, this did not mean that the mother was not respected. Folk-sayings, transmitted from one generation to another for centuries, emphasized the importance of being a credit to one's mother. "Instruction" or "commandment" by one's father is frequently paired with "teaching" by one's mother in such fashion that the two are practically synonymous. (See Proverbs 1:8, 6:20.) Specific laws requiring obedience and respect for one's mother are found in such passages as Exodus 20:12 and Deuteronomy 22:15.

These factors mean that, though the one essential role of the wife/mother was that of bearing children, within the family she was second in authority only to the father. Sons—even mature men of wide experience—were expected to pay deference to their mothers and to yield to their judgment. In this respect, the status of the Biblical mother is poles apart from that of the modern mother who begins to find her children in open rebellion against her authority before they are out of their teens.

Because of her high position, the mother of a king or a prophet was likely to have important influence upon the course of national affairs. Women of low estate as well as high were expected to participate fully in religious ceremonies linked with the great holy periods such as the Passover, Pentecost, and the Feast of Tabernacles. They attended religious festivals and took part in ritualistic acts associated with ceremonial meals and the like.

There are a few Old Testament instances of "prophetic" activity on the part of a woman. This role, usually regarded as reserved for men, was clearly played by Deborah and Miriam as well as "Huldah the prophetess." (See II Kings 22.) In less obvious fashion, the wife of Isaiah seems to have influenced the public messages of her God-intoxicated husband.

Far more important than these conspicuous public functions was the everyday role of the wife-mother-homemaker. Management of day-to-day family activities was largely in her hands.

She taught her sons—informally, it is true, but nonetheless decisively. Through her sons, she influenced the destiny of the family; and through the family, the destiny of the nation.

Small wonder, therefore, that the Bible paints an idealistic picture of "the good woman." She displays self-control and modesty, along with efficiency as a home-maker. She is prudent and trustworthy. Her virtue is far more important to her than fine clothing and jewelry. She is kind, wise, and, above all, God-fearing. Though her life is normally centered in her family and her home so that she does not achieve distinction or fame in her own right, in her heart she knows that she is the strongest force in society because she bears children, nurtures them, and largely directs the course of their lives.

Woman: Instrument of God in Effecting Salvation

Orthodox Christian thought stresses the wholly incredible fact that Jesus Christ, the Saviour of the World, is the Son of God born to a virgin by the agency of the Holy Spirit rather than a human father. Few issues have caused so much ink to be spilled, so uselessly. For there is no doubt that the Gospel writers themselves were vividly aware of the "contradiction" involved in simultaneously describing the miraculous conception of their Lord and tracing his ancestry through Joseph.

This very contradiction stresses "the impossible," namely, that Jesus of Nazareth was at one and the same time entirely divine and fully human. Across the centuries, men and women attempting to follow the compass of Christian thought have tended to waver a few degrees away from due north. No matter how slight such a deviation may be, it destroys the heart of the Gospel message. During some early centuries, the temptation was to minimize the humanity of Jesus by emphasizing the divinity of the ever-living Christ. Today, we face the opposite dilemma. We have made so much of the human Jesus who was the greatest of all teachers and the best of all leaders, that we sometimes fail to fall prostrate before him as the Son of God.

In Jesus Christ, the whole Biblical process comes to a climax. Through his humanity, he is one of us—bone of our bone and flesh of our flesh. Consequently in his self-giving on the Cross, he offers himself as a substitute for us. He takes upon himself our sins, and pays the penalty for our human failures. But he also reaches down to save us, in a cosmic sense, because he is the Son of God as well as the Son of Man.

God used a woman, the Virgin Mary, as the supreme instrument in bringing into the world the Saviour whose coming was foreshadowed in the marriage contract between Jehovah and the Chosen People. Reacting from Roman Catholic excesses in veneration of the Holy Virgin, Protestants have tended to ignore or minimize or sentimentalize her role in the drama of salvation. Restored to her proper place in the epic of God's dealings with mankind and seen as a vital instrument without which God Himself could not have acted as He did, the Virgin Mary gives new dignity to womanhood and to motherhood.

For Discussion

In terms of basic human values, do you think today's "emancipated woman" is more significant than the woman who took second place to the father/husband in Biblical times? Why do you support your conclusion?

In the familiar and beloved King James Version, Luke 2:5 describes the Virgin Mary has having been "great with child." This language has been dropped from the Revised Standard Version because of changes in our patterns of speech. Looking for a moment at Elizabethan language, in this phrase we find ourselves asking what greatness is. In some fashion, one who is great is large, of course. Do you agree or disagree with the view that being "great with child" is potentially more important than playing a large part in community affairs, or winning a great name as an athlete, musician, or leader in the church?

Assuming a desire on the part of both men and women to recapture and strengthen qualities that contribute to the Biblical image of the family, do you think this a hopelessly lost cause or one in which progress can be made? On what do you base your conclusions?

Chapter 5

Children--and the Church in the Home

MOST readers of the New Testament are aware that Luke's Gospel represents a careful attempt to present "an orderly account" (Luke 1:3). Many who have noticed this aspect of the report have failed to discover that once he has completed his introductory statement, Luke begins his story with an account of a strange birth announcement!

Regardless of the interpretation you favor concerning the strange story of the birth of John the Baptist, it is hard to escape the central emphasis of that story. God the Creator sent divine messages to Zechariah regarding it—and this stresses the fact that God is actively concerned with sex and procreation.

God chose so to fashion man that the bringing of new life into being, and its development in the social womb of the family and the community, is too stupendous a process for us to analyze—to say nothing of really "controlling." Regardless of whether or not an angel comes with messages to father or mother, every time a child is conceived God the Creator is actively involved.

Incredibly and wonderfully, God uses sex as an instrument in bringing divine messengers into the world! Hence the whole story of Zechariah and Elizabeth and the son of their old age is a backdrop against which to view the drama of family life. Human reproduction, a colossal miracle in its own right, is a major aspect of continuing divine creation. Any new-born baby, not simply a potential John the Baptist, can be an explosive agent who will contribute to the emergence of the absolutely novel— namely, to the continuing work of divine creation.

It is recognition of this divine element in procreation that led the ancient Hebrews, in their story of Adam and Eve, to stress the fact that every conception is a miracle. This is the sense in which Eve exults that "I have gotten a man with the help of the Lord" (Genesis 4:1).

Given the fearful and wonderful responsibility/opportunity of partaking in ongoing creation through the procreation and rearing of a child, a man and woman function as partners with God. No more wonderful, solemnly important, or ceaselessly difficult role can be imagined. By comparison with parenthood, all other human vocations pale into insignificance.

This point of view, and the scale of values upon which it rests, may be found everywhere in Scripture.

Parenthood the Most Significant Achievement

No matter what high position he might win and what honors he might achieve, the ancient Jew considered himself a failure if he did not have children—including at least one son to perpetuate his name. A saying from the Talmud, which came very close to achieving the status of Scripture, warns quite bluntly: "These four reckon as dead—the blind, the leper, the poor, and the childless." That is, the childless person was in as desperate a situation as any man could enter; there was nothing worse.

Even in very early periods, it was recognized that one can become a father or a mother in non-biological ways. Adoption was practiced even in the period of the patriarchs. (See Genesis 15:2, 3.) A son or daughter brought into the family by this means was as much "flesh of one's flesh, bone of one's bone" as a natural child.

Whether the fruit of adoption or of procreation and birth, every child took part in ceremonies oriented toward God. That is, a baby was not fully "a member of the family" until ceremonially presented to Jehovah and redeemed through long-established rites. In the case of a male child, circumcision was a vital aspect of the act of dedicating the baby and his creative powers to the God who had created him.

Viewed through modern eyes, some of the rites linked with the birth and dedication of a baby were crude—even repulsive. To fasten on their external features is to miss their reason for being: no less than that of serving to convey emotion-charged meaning in such fashion that parents and friends and neighbors will see that birth is a *religious* event.

Regardless of his position on the economic scale and his place in the power structure of his community, any man who had numerous children was regarded as rich and successful. Parenthood gave him a position of influence and dignity.

Responsibilities of Children and of Parents

It is impossible to form a rounded concept of the Biblical image of the family without giving brief attention to the basic point of view that is summarized in Proverbs 22:6:

> Train up a child in the way he should go,
> and when he is old he will not depart from it.

To bring a child into the world or to bring him into the family by adoption and then to engage in ceremonies that stressed God's role in the coming of new life were not enough. Every parent was expected to take his or her sons and daughters as personal responsibilities, and personally to take part in the long process of "training." This training included instruction in ways to go about the ordinary activities of life, of course. For the majority of children it also involved most or all that we now associate with school —absorbing the inherited wisdom from the past and learning how to apply it in the present.

Yet in many respects the most important kind of instruction given a child by his parents was informal rather than formal, and had nothing to do with skill or knowledge. Values by which to live, and goals toward which to direct one's life, were largely imparted through parental influence. For a parent to fail in this area constituted the greatest of all failures.

For their part, children were expected to give complete obedience and unquestioning loyalty to the family—headed by the father. In the famous Ten Commandments, or Decalogue, the first four commandments have to do with one's relationship with God and observance of God's regulations concerning His name and His holy day, the Sabbath. The familiar fifth commandment demands of every son and daughter:

Honor your father and your mother, that your days may be long in the land which the Lord your God gives you (Exodus 20:12).

Subsequent to this fifth commandment and therefore secondary to it in terms of sequence are the regulations that govern community life—forbidding murder, adultery, theft, false witness, and covetousness. Not simply young children and adolescents, but grown men and women were expected to maintain respect for their parents and to follow in their footsteps.

It is this aspect of the child-parent relationship, producing in the child a deeply-ingrained attitude of obedience and trust, that Jesus exalts in his familiar exhortations about the necessity for being childlike in order to enter the Kingdom of God. (See, for example, Mark 10:13-17.) A child of the Kingdom, said the Saviour, must exhibit toward his heavenly father the attitudes ideally associated with the relationship between a child and his father in the flesh.

"The Church in the Home"

Refined and elevated by Jesus, Old Testament teachings about the parent-child relationship had an important bearing on the development of the Christian Church. For in its earliest and simplest form, a "church" was made up of a group of Jesus' followers who tried to conduct themselves as a spiritual family.

Indeed, in a literal and not simply a figurative sense, a husband and wife and a group of children who eagerly put their religious convictions at the center of their family circle, constituted a "church." Seen as one of the most powerful influences that can shape the destiny of a human being, family worship emerges as "important" on a scale seldom fully recognized in our time. In subtle fashion, values have been so altered that many a modern parent quite honestly expects the church school—in all its activities—to assume responsibility for the spiritual training of children.

Without reducing the influence or minimizing the importance of Sunday school, Vacation Bible School, youth fellowship, and the like, perhaps we can recapture the Biblical sense of parental responsibility. It is father and mother, rather than teachers and counselors or even pastors, who must assume responsibility for being sure that their "children are believers and not open to the charge of being profligate or insubordinate" (Titus 1:6).

It is because Jesus takes such responsibility for granted that he speaks of the Church as a family and of disciples or converts as "children of the Kingdom."

FOR DISCUSSION

One of the subtle but significant trends in modern life is that which has led to a gradual reduction in the amount of time a child spends with his parents. Where a father's job requires him to be away from home much of the time, his opportunity to "train up his child in the way he should go" is even less significant than the opportunity of the mother.

In the face of complex working schedules, compulsory education, kindergartens, and day nurseries, what is the modern parent to do? Do you think it still holds true that a father and mother are really responsible for the development of a child's outlook on life and scale of values? Why or why not?

According to prevailing usage in the United States, a "child" is younger than an "adolescent." Among whites of this country, it is an unwritten proverb that "no roof is big enough to cover persons of more than two generations." (This point of view is not nearly so pronounced among Negro Americans.)

Do you think the practice of "cutting the apron-strings" fairly early has contributed to the difficulty of having members of three or four generations living together? Other than trying to make them comfortable in a retirement home or nursing home, what responsibility do modern adults have for their aging parents?

Chapter 6

Adultery

IF YOU will turn in your Revised Standard Version of the New Testament to the seventh chapter of John, you will find a passage pulled from context and printed at the bottom of the page in miniature italic type.

The story of Jesus' dealings with "a woman who had been caught in adultery" (John 7:53–8:11) is one of the most fascinating and revealing passages in the entire Scriptural record.

Translators of the Revised Standard Version made a sort of footnote of the story because it does not appear in the oldest manuscripts of the New Testament. It was used in the Fourth Century Latin Bible prepared by Jerome and famous in Christian history as the Vulgate because it was written in "vulgar" Latin as opposed to learned and scholarly Latin. Until our own time, most translations of Scripture were based directly or indirectly upon the Vulgate. As a result, the famous King James Version treats the encounter with the woman taken in adultery as an organic part of the sacred text.

Why this state of confusion?

Our earliest and most complete Greek manuscripts of the New Testament make no mention of the sinful woman whom irate authorities dragged before Jesus for judgment. Even the manuscripts that include the story vary in their handling of it. In some, it appears at the end of John's Gospel. In others, it is inserted after Luke 21:38, where it becomes the final and most emotion-packed incident in a series involving Jesus' indictment of "big wheels" in the religious institution of his day.

Jerome obviously considered this strange story to be genuine Holy Writ, else he would not have included it in the Vulgate. Though he died more than fifteen centuries ago, he still ranks among the foremost scholars of all time. Both St. Augustine and St. Ambrose, who was bishop of Milan in the Fourth Century, were acquainted with the account in spite of the fact that it appeared in only a few manuscripts that have survived. The father of church history, Eusebius of Caesarea, said that very soon after the close of the Apostolic Age, there was in circulation a "Gospel of the Hebrews" that included an incident whose echoes are reminiscent of those from the story of the adulteress.

What are we to make of this state of affairs?

Some Biblical scholars think the nature of the account led to its deletion from early manuscripts. Augustine himself reported that it was "a source of scandal to some of slight faith." For if you will re-read the vivid story, you will see that on the surface —only on the surface—it seems to offer comfort to those who engage in sexual promiscuity. In the turbulent years when the new faith about a crucified and risen Saviour was spreading from Palestine into the Graeco-Roman world, notorious for gross immorality, it was probably dangerous to offer even the slightest comfort to Christians who engaged in adultery. So the story of Jesus' dealing with a tainted woman may have circulated by word of mouth rather than in writing.

Pause now and read it for yourself, once or several times, before we proceed to examine the Biblical view concerning adultery. ("The Woman Taken in Adultery" is the central figure in John 7:53–8:11.)

Violent Views Expressed in the Old Testament

Among the ancient People of the Covenant, adultery held a prominent place in the list of social sins. It is condemned in both the Seventh and the Tenth Commandments and figured in a great many laws governing guilt and punishment.

Any bride who was found not to be a virgin was judged unworthy not simply for matrimony, but for life; she was condemned to be stoned (Deuteronomy 22:13-21). Because chastity was a life-or-death matter, any man who violated a girl was compelled to marry her.

Stoning was considered too good for the daughter of a priest who played the harlot; she was supposed to be burned to death (Leviticus 21:9). A betrothed damsel violated by force was spared, but willing adultery involving a married or betrothed woman carried a death penalty for both parties.

Some scholars think that the extreme penalty was seldom carried out. You recall, however, that Jesus' clash with Temple authorities centered in the fact that men who considered themselves pure and guiltless had picked up stones with which to pelt a woman "caught in the act" and, therefore, unquestionably guilty.

Sexual purity, as defined in modern thought, was not the only issue involved in the Old Testament prohibitions of adultery. Earlier, we saw that absolute authority of the father over other members of the family involved concepts very close to "ownership." As a result, adultery was both a moral violation and an offense against property. Written and unwritten codes specified that every man has sole right to sexual possession of his wife, and that every father has the right to be sure that children borne by his wife "belong to him" and no one else.

Especially in the period of the patriarchs, this scheme of values that sounds so strange to us produced some results we would prefer not to think about. Property rights centering in males and sexual union being a vital property right, not all extra-marital acts of copulation constituted "adultery." A man who took a female slave who was not betrothed was not guilty of a grave offense. Even if he violated a damsel of his own people, offense against the property rights of the girl's father was a more serious matter than that of offense to the young woman herself.

Loose as some laws were by present standards, adultery was a common and persistent problem. Moral laxity was a favorite topic for denunciations of the prophets—those God-intoxicated men who felt themselves called to awaken the conscience of society. Part of the glory of the Bible lies precisely here. It is not a pretty-pretty story that depicts mankind in idealistic terms. Rather, it is a grimly realistic account of a particular group of people who were in a special relationship with the one high God and as a result were eternally suffering pangs of guilt for their misdoings —sexual and otherwise.

Adultery Redefined by Jesus

Without relaxing the severity of denunciations for those who broke laws concerning chastity, Jesus gave fresh depth to the term. With one bold sweep he did away with the demand for respect of a father's or a husband's property rights and underscored purity as an ideal in its own right.

"You have heard that it was said, 'You shall not commit adultery.' But I say to you that every one who looks at a woman lustfully has already committed adultery with her in his heart" (Matthew 5:27-28).

Redefined in this fashion, adultery becomes a violation of personality in the name of lust and ranks high on the list of those socially condemned acts that are also sins against God the Creator. Writers of New Testament letters are urgent and vivid in their condemnation of this new kind of adultery. (See Romans 13:9, Galatians 5:19, and James 2:11, for example.)

Instead of making "the law of Moses" null and void, Jesus gave it new life and spirit by elevating it to a higher plane. This issue was at the heart of the violent clash in which he defended an obviously guilty woman from the attacks of Temple authorities. His treatment of her case involved pardon for the sinner, without in any way condoning her sin. In the process of arguing for such a conclusion, the Messiah boldly asserted that every man among her accusers was also tainted with sin—guilty of the new adultery that consists of harboring lustful thoughts or feeding the eye on voluptuous sights even if absolutely free of contamination from overt sexual union with a woman other than one's wife.

Defined in the incredibly radical fashion of Jesus, adultery emerges as one of the flagrant public sins of our time. For those who have merchandise to sell have concluded that prospective buyers can be attracted by using sex as bait. As a result, ours is perhaps the most sex-soaked culture ever to exist. Even though multitudes remain physically pure, no one can function in our society without being exposed to a constant barrage of insistent invitations to sin by means of the eye.

It is at least interesting, and it may be important, that only in the account of the woman taken in adultery do we have any indication that Jesus ever wrote anything. And what he wrote on that occasion, we do not know! Some Greek manuscripts of the Gospel of John include an explanatory phrase: "He wrote on the ground the sins of every one of them."

We may as well be honest with ourselves and admit that, if absolute purity is taken as the standard demand of us, Jesus Christ would have little trouble writing on the ground a long list of my sins and yours.

Strangely—and wonderfully—it is precisely here that, in our survey of "The Biblical Image of the Family," we come face to face with our own need for the acceptance of the Good News. Jesus Christ came into the world to save sinners. If every other area of life were left unconsidered, we would quickly find ourselves sinners by surveying our attitudes toward sex. It is out of a sense of need that we cry for help; it is as a result of receiving a conviction after a just trial that we ask for mercy.

Challenged by experts in the law, the Saviour condemned the sins of a stained woman—and simultaneously forgave the sinner. In doing so, he reinforced his insistent and persistent emphasis on the fact that victory in the race of life comes as a result of divine rescue and not as a result of flexing one's own muscles. However it may be defined in the courts, the adultery that consists of any transgression by means of deed, word, look, or thought serves to condemn each of us and to revive in us an urgent sense of longing for divine rescue.

FOR DISCUSSION

Do you consider our present age to be "better" or "worse" in the sight of God than earlier epochs? What led you to this conclusion? What evidence, from secular sources and from Scripture, can you offer to support your verdict? In terms of your own everyday life and your relationship with God, what are the consequences of the point of view you support?

Chapter 7
Divorce

REGARDLESS of what anyone may say about "the alarming rise in the U.S. divorce rate," there is no accurate way of making comparisons between different cultures and various periods. This is because divorce (and separation) have been defined quite differently in different epochs. Any statistical comparison between, say, the divorce rate in medieval France and modern America is meaningless.

For the heart of the legal process of divorce is that of cutting in two the organic entity that has been formed by union of man and wife. Divorce is only one method of arriving at that conclusion. Separation, desertion, and mutual neglect or mutual infidelity by agreement, while preserving a legal marriage, produce many of the end results that are achieved more swiftly and perhaps more publicly by divorce.

So the first basic reality to be faced in a survey of divorce rests in the fact that, wherever marriage has been practiced, men and women have devised ways of making that marriage ineffective or void. Actual customs guiding the process of divorce, and public attitudes toward them, have of course varied widely. It is strange and startling to recognize at this point that there has been total reversal between ancient Jewish and modern American divorce customs at one important point.

Today it is generally taken for granted that divorce action will be instituted by the wife—regardless of whether or not she is the partner who insists that the union must be severed. Among the people used by God in bringing the Bible into existence and the Saviour into history, almost without exception a divorce action was brought about by the husband.

A Startling and Sobering Survey

Regardless of how modern Christians treat marriage and divorce in actual practice, the principle of the sanctity of marriage is almost universally accepted. In the light of that principle, it is startling and sobering to discover that the Old Testament takes divorce quite for granted. This is an aspect of Scripture we would rather not talk about—and an emphasis with which we must wrestle honestly if we are to emerge with a rounded and workable understanding of "The Biblical Image of the Family."

Among the peoples from whom the Hebrew patriarchs came, it was the traditional right of a husband to "put away" his wife. This principle was retained by Abraham, Isaac, Jacob, and their descendants. A classic example is that of Abraham, who sent Hagar and his wife and Ishmael his son into the desert. He took that course of action in desperation, as a way to relieve family tensions that had developed because Sarah and Hagar quarreled with one another.

Christian piety tends to gloss over this vivid story, reported in considerable detail in Genesis 21, on the basis of the fact that Hagar was a "concubine" and not a "wife." She was, of course, a foreigner—an Egyptian, to be precise—and a slave. But no interpretation can avoid facing the fact that Abraham took Hagar to himself with the hope that she would bear him a son to perpetuate his name and blood. So viewed, his union with Hagar was as fully a "marriage" as was his union with Sarah in a period when polygamy was common.

The truth is that Abraham simply acted in keeping with the age-old tradition—still very much alive in the time of Jesus—according to which a husband could put away his wife just about any time he chose to do so, for any reason he cared to name.

Leviticus, or "The Book of the Levitical Priesthood," makes it very clear that divorce was common in ancient times. Prescribing the proper marital status for priests, it directed that, "They shall not marry a harlot or a woman who has been defiled; neither shall they marry a woman divorced from her husband; for the priest is holy to his God" (Leviticus 21:7). Similar references to divorced women in Leviticus 21:14, 22:13, Numbers 30:9 and other ancient passages make it abundantly clear that among the early Hebrews divorce was actual and not simply theoretical.

A man could send away his wife if she failed to bear him a son, if she proved unfaithful to him, if she created family friction (as in the case of Hagar), or for practically any other reason he wished to advance. To make the dissolution of the union "legal," the husband customarily prepared a certificate or "bill" of divorce. Necessarily brief because writing materials were scarce, a document of this sort is perhaps preserved or reflected in Hosea 2:2:

> She is not my wife,
> and I am not her husband.

For additional light on this practice and that of sending away the wife, see: Deuteronomy 24:1-4, Isaiah 50:1, Jeremiah 3:8. Some of these passages suggest that husband and wife may have appeared before a public official who saw and could attest that the bill of divorce had actually been delivered to the woman.

For her part, the wife had no legal redress. She could attempt to persuade her husband—but was helpless to stop him if he made up his mind that they should part company. In the strange reversal that has occurred in contemporary Christian society, it is the wife who can bring a marriage to an end if she wishes. Even against the violent protests of her partner, any woman who really wants a divorce can get it—whether on the grounds of tangible infidelity or intangible "mental cruelty."

Jesus Faces the Issue of Divorce

Generations of Jewish scholars added a great many interpretations and comments to their body of law which included all the elements we now separate into the compartments of criminal law, civil law, and moral law. On many issues, separate "schools of thought" developed. Such was the case with adultery. By the First Century, b.c., the Hillel school taught that the "indecency" which constitutes grounds for divorce (Deuteronomy 24:1) covers a broad spectrum of conduct. Against this view, the Shammai school insisted that only adultery constitutes indecency and hence that no other basis for divorce is valid.

Pharisees who were well aware of these conflicting views probably hoped to trap Jesus when they "tested him" by inquiring whether or not it is lawful (right in the sight of God) to divorce one's wife for any cause (Matthew 19:3). Jesus' answer to this loaded question constitutes one of his most important statements on the subject of divorce—and the family:

He answered, "Have you not read that he who made them from the beginning made them male and female, and said, 'For this reason a man shall leave his father and mother and be joined to his wife, and the two shall become one'? So they are no longer two but one. What therefore God has joined together, let no man put asunder." They said to him, "Why then did Moses command one to give a certificate of divorce, and to put her away?" He said to them, "For your hardness of heart Moses allowed you to divorce your wives, but from the beginning it was not so. And I say to you: whoever divorces his wife, except for unchastity, and marries another, commits adultery" (Matthew 19:4-9).

In modern times, few phrases of the New Testament have been more hotly debated than the qualifying clause of the final sentence, "except for unchastity." While this same exception permitting re-marriage of one justifiably divorced appears in Matthew 5:32, it is missing from such vital statements as those of Mark 10:11-12 and Luke 16:18. Many interpreters hold that the comparatively "relaxed" law of Matthew is the result of a late editorial change by a scribe copying a manuscript, who felt that the "absolute" law against remarriage after divorce was unrealistic and could never be enforced. Support for those who hold such a view is afforded by the edicts of Paul, especially the famous statements concerning marriage in his First Letter to the Corinthians.

Here, space permits a hasty look at only one aspect of our Lord's system of values and laws of conduct. Regardless of how one may interpret a controversial passage such as that of Matthew 19:9, an "over view" of the Gospel record makes it indisputably clear that Jesus regarded marriage as a mysterious and sublime merging of two persons into one. That is, he saw marriage as a *union* and not as a legal contract depending for its importance upon the written and unwritten laws of the community. Moreover, Jesus held firmly to the view that marriage is *permanent* and not temporary; it is a mystical state which, once entered, is not subject to dissolution. In this sense, a man and woman who have become one in marriage can never dissolve the organic entity they have created, even though they may be divorced and go their separate ways.

That is, Jesus saw marriage as *the merging of two lives to form "a new creation, under God."*

Such a view was just as strange and just as convicting to the Jews of the First Century as to the Christians of the Twentieth. It has power and validity only to the degree that men see in Jesus of Nazareth the eternal Son of God, fully human and totally divine at one and the same time and demonstrated to be such by the central act of history: his resurrection from the grave.

Here we see that one's theology, however formally or informally it has been formed, is the final determining factor in arriving at a Christian interpretation of divorce. If Jesus was simply "the greatest of all moral teachers," then we are likely to endorse those interpretations which make his demands relatively easy. But if he rose from the grave in order to conquer sin and death to effect rescue for you and for me, then we must be prepared to accept hard sayings and impossible demands from him.

An Act of Self-examination

Remembering that it is possible to stumble by means of a lust-born look as well as by overt acts, examine your life to arrive at a self-inventory. In what ways have you violated the principles of Jesus and jeopardized the stability of your family? Be specific. Call names of parents, brothers and sisters, husband or wife, children and grand-children. Try to dwell on each name long enough to form a clear mental image of the face that goes with it. In each instance, examine your conduct and attitude as a prelude to making a mental list of your offenses.

After half an hour, what do you think of yourself? What can you do about things in the distant past or the immediate past? How will you find forgiveness for your guilt, and strength to start over?

Chapter 8

Family Enrichment through Use of the Bible

CHRISTENDOM has gone through many, many different epochs in terms of the general attitude toward Scripture. During early generations of the Church, the holy book to which Jesus' followers turned when they needed a formal written guide was, of course, our Old Testament. It is particularly interesting and thrilling to notice in the letters of Paul that his whole missionary message and his entire evangelistic career grew out of "nothing more" than familiarity with the Old Testament plus the personal experience of encounter with the resurrected Christ.

Obviously, that "nothing more" is actually all-encompassing. You and I could make the same spiritual odyssey as Paul, if we had to do so. Our own pilgrimage is made infinitely more thrilling and satisfying because we have the New Testament to amplify and interpret the Old Testament.

There were, however, generations during which the gradual crystalization of the New Testament was still taking place. During this period, individual Christians and Councils of the

Church read, listened, interpreted, and debated as to whether or not a particular document should be considered as Scripture.

When the formal list, or "canon," of the New Testament was made and its contents added to the Old Testament, there were generations—if not centuries—of avid excitement. By our standards, copies were incredibly scarce and expensive. Hence a person who had an opportunity to read the Bible (or portions of it) considered this a rare and thrilling experience. The sacred text was likely to be approached with excitement and longing; to read Scripture, or hear it read, was an emotional experience.

You remember, of course, the general story of how Christianity became the "official" religion of a Roman Empire that was still largely pagan. And you recall how the fall of the political empire left the Church with great power and wealth, with the result that during the long centuries before the rise of modern European nations the Church paid less and less attention to the Bible, more and more attention to preserving its wealth and guarding its ceremonies.

Though Martin Luther took from Paul's Letter to the Romans a phrase, "justification by faith," and used it as the battle-cry of the Reformation, he might as logically have said simply, "back to the Bible!" For the Reformation set the authority of the Bible and one's interpretation of it against the authority of tradition, the religious institution, and holy ceremonies.

Puritans and other religious minority groups who played so important a part in founding the United States were still glowing with the fires of Luther. It was for this reason that the Bible played so vital a part in shaping the courses of families, individual lives, and through them the philosophy of the new nation.

As late as 1900, the practice of reading from the Bible and praying together was central to the religious experience of many Americans. In some sections of the nation and among some families, it continued to be a vital practice until well after World War I.

But the authority of Scripture was challenged both by the "new Biblical scholarship" that centered chiefly in Germany and by the rise of the physical sciences. Beginning about 1920, challenges directed toward the significance of the Bible multiplied in tempo and ferocity. Part of the effectiveness of these challenges grew out of the fact that "the faithful" were not content simply to defend Scripture as God's inspired word. Many went so far as to insist that the King James (or Authorized) Version of 1611 is the one and only authentic Holy Book of Christendom and to declare that its words are to be accepted and not interpreted.

This point of view, unfortunately, received a label. It is commonly known as "fundamentalism."

More than any other one factor since the Reformation, the controversy between "fundamentalism" and "liberalism" split and injured the Protestant wing of Christendom. But almost before the first angry words were spoken, other less obvious forces were at work.

Scientific archaeology, launched just a bit more than a century ago, has proved an incredibly rich field of endeavor. Scholars now know far more about the cultural epochs from which sections of the Bible came than did men during any previous period of history. Streams of vivid, readable, and inspiring books are pouring from the printing presses. Here are just a few that fall in the category we have been discussing: Madeleine S. and J. Lane Miller, *Encyclopedia of Bible Life* (Harper, 1955); Nelson Beecher Keyes, *Story of the Bible World* (The Reader's Digest Association, 1962); *Illustrated World of the Bible Library*, five volumes (McGraw-Hill Book Co., 1958); Michael Avi-Yonah and Emil G. Kraeling, *Our Living Bible*, a condensed version of the five-volume set listed just above (McGraw-Hill Book Co., 1962); G. S. Wegener, *6,000 Years of the Bible* (Harper & Row, 1963); and, of course, *The Interpreter's Dictionary of the Bible* in four volumes (Abingdon Press, 1962). Many, many other useful books in this general category could be listed. More good ones have been published in the last twenty years than during the previous 2,000 years.

Along with progress in archaeology and the understanding of ancient life and thought, there has been a corresponding rise of interest in translating the Bible. Some modern versions are "official" ones, endorsed by large Christian bodies. Others are "private" ones, issued because the translator and publisher felt they would meet important needs. More worthy translations of Scripture have been published since 1920, by four or five times, than during the entire period from the Reformation until World War I.

As a result of these and other factors, you and I are living in a time radically different from that of the "doubting twenties." There is a widespread and a wholesome "return to the Bible," far removed from the spirit of fundamentalism that merely seeks to cling to the past in order to avoid genuinely coming to grips with the present. In this new spirit and with multiplied resources with which to work, every modern family can make the Bible "come alive" and serve as both map and compass for each member.

Employ Some of the Tools Available

If your family is to be a Bible-oriented family in the best sense of the word, you will certainly have to make use of some tools. Interests will vary widely according to age and experience, of course. But for everyone, from toddlers just learning to sit still a few minutes and listen, to grandparents troubled by having "too much time on their hands," splendid books are available. Some of them may be secured from your public library. The rank and file of church folk pay taxes to support city or county libraries, but seldom use them. You will find librarians eager to help you, and ready to supply many good books. If your local church has a library, you will probably find that it includes many helpful books about the Bible, Biblical archaeology, and what the Bible means, as well as translations with which you are not familiar.

After exploring a bit, you will certainly want to buy some books for your own family. From the money you would spend for a couple of nights at the drive-in theater or one day at the beach, you can get weeks or months of satisfaction by investing in books that interest and challenge you. If you own only one translation of the Bible (or of the New Testament), you will want to investigate others and become familiar with them even if you remain wedded to the familiar language of your old favorite.

Let the Whole Family Participate

Regardless of age ranges involved, try to use your God-given ingenuity to devise ways to involve every member of the family in a continuous exposure to the "irradiation of meaning and value" that is the unique function of the Bible. In the case of small children, you may find Bible stories helpful. But if the practice is started early, surprisingly young boys and girls will at least sit still while the Bible itself is read by father or mother.

That is to say, there is no escape from discipline, no "happy formula" by which a family can have all the benefits that are to be derived from using the Bible together without being willing to pay the price in terms of time and interest. But the element of "you must" can be greatly reduced by imaginative leadership. By regularly approaching the Bible as a source of joy and a guidebook for the next step of life's journey, members of a family look forward to their time with the Book as a period of pleasure and not drudgery.

Spend Some Time with the Bible Itself

Commentaries, study materials, Bible stories, and books about life in Bible times are interesting and often essential. But the family needs to spend some time with the Bible itself. A single paragraph, read aloud by one member of the family and then discussed for even a quarter of an hour, will literally "come alive." Children too small to participate in such an activity will enter it naturally and normally if their parents and older brothers or sisters have habitually followed it in their presence.

By all means, do investigate some of the "modern" translations. Each translator or group of translators has a distinctive personality (just as there are wide differences among the Gospel writers themselves). Some styles and treatments will appeal to some persons, while others will prove more attractive to another member of the family. Always, however, without exception, when an individual or a family approaches an unfamiliar translation with an open mind and eager heart, fresh insights will be gained. Whether you "like" it or not, you cannot read Luke's Gospel in *The New English Bible* without being jerked up short many times. Its vivid language simply will not slip through the mind without striking some sparks.

In this exciting and provocative and central area of Christian thought and experience, perhaps the guiding rule should be simply: *do something.* We are prone to pay homage to the Bible; to give it a kind of attention in public worship and in church school study; to say, "Yes, we'd like to do something with the Bible in our family"; and then do nothing. So the most important single principle offered here is that of making an actual start upon some type of Bible-centered experience for the whole family. Do something, even if in a week you decide it is not right and you have to modify the program you drew up in advance!

Chapter 9

A Source-Book for Solving Family Problems

HAPPY families are all alike; every unhappy family is unhappy in its own way."

Leo Tolstoy's terse characterization, with which he opens his account of the spiritual decay of Anna Karenina, is clearly too simple. Yet it has a degree of validity.

For in order to be happy, a family must have a basic set of goals more or less clearly defined and accepted by each member of the family. In addition, a happy family must have a practical means of resolving those inevitable personal tensions that build up from time to time even between two (or three, or eight) individuals who under most circumstances would literally die for one another.

Scripture fulfills both conditions.

During generations in which the Bible was a major focus of family loyalty and interest, it is likely that in many households the Word of God helped to produce genuine happiness without deliberate striving for this effect. Husbands and wives read the

Bible themselves and taught their children from it, simply because this was a way of life in which they themselves had been reared. They did not turn to Scripture as a tool with which to resolve family tensions and a compass with which to chart individual and group journeys through life. They did not have to do that deliberately or as a result of floundering around for a source of help. For many persons in the epoch when Bible reading and family prayer were taken for granted, effects came as unsought dividends.

With occasional conspicuous exceptions, today's family, whose members are active participants in the program of a middle-class or upper-class congregation, fail to receive unplanned and unsought dividends from the use of the Bible in the home. For as has been noted earlier, the fires on the family altar have burned low and the Bible is virtually an unknown Book to great numbers of persons today.

In order, then, to gain the twofold set of benefits by which the Bible helps resolve family problems, it must be used regularly and faithfully over long periods of time. Whether or not any of the specific suggestions offered in Chapter 8 appeal to you and your family, you must adopt the point of view presented there and develop a pattern of spiritual discipline if the Bible is to have practical, everyday impact upon your life.

Long-range effects of individual and family striving for dialogue with God through His Book fall into two great categories: the shaping of goals and values and the impact upon pressing and urgent problems.

1. Scripture Influences Your View of What Is Important

Brief individual passages and favorite memory verses will help you to select a high goal and to continue moving toward it, of course. But over a period of years these fragments from Scripture are not so important or influential in this respect as is the basic viewpoint that is common to every part of the Bible.

Poems, letters, hero tales, accounts of the life and message of Jesus, dry and barren books giving obscure details of Jewish history, psalms, parables, and miracles are astonishingly alike in spite of their differences. For throughout the Bible, there are underlying assumptions—sometimes brought to the surface and made quite explicit—whose acceptance or rejection will greatly affect the nature of one's life.

Life has purpose and meaning, asserts the Book. Organic matter on an obscure planet in a solar system of minor size did not come into being either by chance or by the operation of impersonal "laws of nature." On the contrary, a purposeful Creator who was all-powerful and all-wise, then as well as now, deliberately launched the stream of life.

Furthermore, before the first one-cell organism came into existence, the Creator and Sustainer of all life "purposed in his heart" to shape a unique creature who would be stamped with "the divine image." This view of the nature and meaning of man does not depend upon acceptance of ideas that are incompatible with the best scientific knowledge available.

On the contrary, good religion and good science are active partners. It is only when faith degenerates into superstition or science is elevated into an idol that science and religion clash.

Always, under all circumstances, the intangibles of faith must be expressed in language and thought-forms that "make sense" to those who hear. Ancient Hebrews would have rejected as utterly unintelligible any account of the creation of the world and man that used the terms of modern astronomy, physics, and biology. Hence every long-range look at Scripture involves a willingness to go beyond the actual words that are used and to seek the meanings to which these words point. When that is done, the most intelligent and highly educated person of modern times can read the Bible "from Genesis to Revelation" and find no intellectual difficulties to bar him as he seeks to discover from the Book what the universe and life are really like.

Really to accept the doctrines of purposeful divine creation and the dignity of man—and not simply to give lip-service to these ideas too big for our little heads—is to enter a lighted room. For these doctrines imply hope, purpose, and meaning. Neither the frenzies of Baal-worshippers nor the imperial might of Babylon, neither the global spread of communism nor the shadow of the atomic bomb *even so much as touch the fringes of the garments of one who is a pilgrim toward the Eternal City.* Nothing—absolutely nothing—can bring him to despair or to defeat, for by an act of faith he has accepted the supremacy of hope, purpose, and meaning.

Of course, the Biblical story is long and tangled. It involves the (to us) wholly arbitrary choice by God of a queer band of ancient nomads. It includes the complex and sometimes baffling story of the way these Chosen People reacted to their destiny. And it reveals to us how the social womb of the Jewish nation served to nurture and bring forth one who was both Son of Man and Son of God. Finally and decisively, the Bible reveals that through the deliberate self-giving of Jesus Christ, God did for us what we cannot do for ourselves and thereby offered victory to every person who will accept it.

Such sublime ideas are not without paradox and mystery. Neither can they be whittled down to fit neatly inside a man's head, so he can say that he "understands" them in the same way he understands arithmetic or chemistry. But long-range exposure to the Bible gradually enables one to lose sight of the trees and see the forest, to rise above proof-texts and brief quotations into the exhilarating atmosphere of trust in an all-wise God through whom one may seize hold of hope, meaning, and victory.

By influencing your view of what is important and what is eternally significant, the Bible will, over a period of months and years, greatly affect the course of your individual life and the development of your family.

2. Scripture Provides Insight into Present Problems

If you were going into court, you would not think of having your case argued without careful preparation. But some persons decide to make their plea before the bench of Almighty God on the spur of the moment.

There's not much hope of getting a clear answer from on high until you have formulated a precise set of questions. When you are troubled or perplexed or burdened or defeated, observe a period of silence. Try to free your mind of all thoughts whatever, and relax as you lean on the everlasting arms.

Once your mind is comparatively free of stabbing anxieties and blinding frustrations, engage in a period of prayer. If at all possible, get down on your knees. Tell God about your situation just as spontaneously as you would talk to your most intimate friend.

Include in your prayer the fervent petition: "God, send me a message!"

Repeat this plea, or some equivalent of it, many times during your period of wrestling with the presentation of your needs. Continue in this mood until you enter a state of assurance that somehow, soon, the Lord of the universe will give you at least a tiny cue or clue that will serve as an opening through which to move forward toward understanding or decision or forgiveness.

With your case clearly and fervently presented to God and your whole mood one of eager expectancy, turn to the Bible. Read as though it were written for you alone, in your present situation. Spend at least half an hour, without interruption, with some portion of the book that conveys Good News from beginning to end.

If you are a veteran reader of the Bible, perhaps you will have favorite sections that you will wish to reread. If you are a beginner, you may find one of the gospels or a section of the Book of Psalms especially helpful. But the selection of a passage to read is not nearly so important as actually reading it.

Whatever you do, plunge in!

On every page, look for guidance, hints, answers to questions. Read with the breathless hope that the very next line or even a phrase or single word will hit you between the eyes. When it does, you will "know" that you have the divine answer to a pressing personal problem.

Precisely the same approach can be used with the entire family participating. With each member of the family alert for clues and signals that bear upon a dilemma or a decision that must be met, "answers" will emerge in totally unexpected places. Such answers, in turn, will set off family discussion that will proceed at a rate and toward a goal quite different from those involved in "a family conference" not involving the Bible as a problem-solving resource.

Individually and in your family life, try to reject the idea of the impossible. In all your searching and striving, never cease to reach out your hand to take God's envelopes. He is continually sending messages to all of us. But most of us are too busy or too complacent or too self-centered or too frightened to notice when the divine postman knocks at the door of the mind.

Discard the whole notion of "a problem that can't be solved." Rejoice that God is utterly unlimited and can do anything for you and yours . . . now!

Chapter 10

The Christian Family in the Community

NOT ONLY is it impossible for a family to be Christian in isolation; it cannot even exist without organic ties with the society that surrounds and includes it.

In this respect, the Christian family is like the Church. It must be in the world, but not of it. Without severing those bonds that are essential to social existence, both the Church and the family must be guided and shaped by ideals that are not necessarily accepted by a majority of persons within a culture—even when that culture is called a "Christian" nation.

Hastily, let us examine some specific areas in which the Christian family faces vexatious problems and in which some crucial decisions must be made.

1. Inter-faith Marriage

Here, the Biblical emphasis is clear and unequivocal. From the beginning of the strange "marriage bond" between Jehovah and Israel, the people who were self-consciously different from

59

their neighbors were emphatic in discouraging intermarriage with foreigners. This was upon religious grounds, not racial or cultural ones. A worshipper of the one true God who compounded a marriage with a partner who bowed down to idols was in great danger of yielding a bit here and conceding a bit there, eventually becoming less than a faithful follower of Jehovah.

It was for this reason that inter-faith marriage was always discouraged and often flatly forbidden. Marriage between a Jew and a Canaanite was especially likely to bring about spiritual disaster, so it was prohibited by law. (See Deuteronomy 7:1-3, Deuteronomy 23:3, Exodus 34:15.)

Marriage with a captured enemy was permitted under the early code of Abraham's descendants, but could be entered only after suitable rites and ceremonies had been performed (Deuteronomy 21:10-14). The requirement that a "foreign woman" should shave her head and pare her nails was far more drastic than it appears to modern eyes. Among many ancient peoples, including the Hebrews, such fragments of one's body were considered to be of utmost importance. From the perspective of our day, we are tempted to look on the ritual that preceded marriage with a foreign woman as one calculated to guarantee her complete subjection. That was undoubtedly a factor, but by shaving her head and cutting her nails she literally "separated herself" from the people of her birth—and gave up their gods.

Returning to Jerusalem after the Babylonian Exile, the prophet Nehemiah went beyond the requirements of the old law and demanded that true worshippers of Jehovah cease to marry foreign women under any circumstances. Somewhat later, Ezra the scribe revived the old law of Exodus 34:15 and actually established a divorce court whose principal function was that of annulling inter-faith marriages.

While the question of whether or not a worshipper of Jehovah should enter into a union with a mate who burned incense before idols is not a major one today, it is by no means dead. American soldiers stationed in Japan, India, and China and attracted to non-Christian women have had to face this question—and have answered it in various ways.

On a far larger scale, members of the Christian family in the United States must seriously ask, "How far can one go outside the pattern of family belief and worship and achieve a workable marriage?" Methodists and other Protestants live in a social context that includes both non-believers (actually followers of such idols as materialism, comfort, and the like) and active constituents of other religious bodies. Great spiritual risks are attached to marriage outside the faith, and any chasm such as that which separates Protestant Christians from Catholic ones creates hazards not to be taken lightly.

2. Leisure Time

With continuing reduction of the length of time spent in earning a living, modern America faces a crisis at the point of leisure. Leisure constitutes both an opportunity and a problem; used affectively it will enrich individual and family life but abused it will aggravate a great many ills.

Organized religion may well face the greatest crisis since the time Christians constituted a minority group within a frankly pagan society. For the work pattern by which "the week end" has come to dominate the importance of the Sabbath for many persons and family groups is a growing threat to our whole pattern of belief and worship. For practical purposes, Sunday is often the last day of a wholly secular week, rather than the first day of a week consciously entered with confession, praise, and thanksgiving to the God who made and sustains us.

Quite aside from the fundamental spiritual issues that are involved in using "the week end" as a time for pleasure and thereby gnawing away at the strength of the Sabbath, there are practical questions that affect almost every family. Unless leisure time is in some fashion utilized for creative and growth-inducing pursuits, in the end it becomes a curse instead of a blessing. Goals and values are gradually altered when constantly increasing stretches of leisure are used chiefly for self-gratification. Hence as a culture, modern America faces demonic pressures of a type and on scale unlike those to which people of any earlier epoch have been subjected. Whatever creative solutions emerge must be rooted in the Church and in the family.

3. The Working Mother

Most groups of Christians see no moral issue in the question of whether or not a young mother should be employed outside her home. Though there are conspicuous and vocal exceptions, for the most part the contemporary family accepts the conclusion, "Mother has to work because we need the money she makes."

This answer completely by-passes the basic question: "What happens to the children? Who is most influential in giving values, goals, and standards to growing boys and girls?"

In many, many cases—not all—that answer is clear. Baby-sitters, day-school teachers, and others actually spend more hours per day with a child than does his or her mother. Often the arrangements for the children are governed by convenience, rather than by any understanding of the moral and spiritual outlook of the nurse, baby-sitter, or nursery attendant.

More than any other single factor in our time, the increase in the number of working mothers threatens the break down of the family as the primary unit of society.

Few mothers who have adopted this practice or are contemplating it have actually made up a "balance sheet" of gains and losses from working outside the home. Even the net financial gain to the family is far less than many realize. Taking into account taxes, lunches, extra clothing, and other costs, many working mothers are adding very little to the family budget. Even when the net increase is substantial, it may be ear-marked for a second automobile, a ranch-style home, or some other material thing that is desirable by standards of our culture but by no means essential to effective family life.

This subject is so explosive, so emotion-charged that it is often difficult even to get intelligent discussion of it. But no other aspect of the family's relationship to the larger community is more vital than that of whether or not it is right and worth-while for a mother to work outside the home during the formative years when the characters of her children are being formed.

Scripture offers no direct light upon the question of the working mother, for the cultures from which portions of Scripture came were not plagued with this problem. It is only by implication and by inference that we can get Biblical guidance here, in terms of long-range goals and values.

4. The Problem of the Aging

Quite a different situation prevails in relation to the problem of the aging. Scripture is pervaded with direct injunctions to honor one's elders, and throughout its pages the Bible stresses the importance of respecting age.

Modern America, refusing to honor age for age's sake, is the cultural base for a new and frightening development in human affairs. For to all practical purposes, we have about reached a point of view according to which there is no place in the home for members of "the older generation." There are frequent conspicuous exceptions to this view, of course. But as a nation we are entering—if we have not indeed already entered—a climate in which we take it for granted that the aging and the sick should have institutional rather than home care.

No solution is in sight. For developments in medicine and public health point to continued gradual lengthening of the life span—along with continued gradual lowering of mandatory retirement age in industry and business. There is no possible way to build, equip, and staff enough good institutions to take care of the constantly increasing number of persons who feel they have no place as functioning members of a three- or four-generation family.

5. Illness, Tragedy, and Death

The Biblical image of the family depicts a close-knit group of persons who are held together not only by blood bonds and the customs of society, but most important of all, by common belief in and allegiance to God the Father, God the Son, and God the Holy Spirit.

That is to say, the family whose ideal we find in the pages of Scripture is equipped to meet the heartaches and heartbreaks that cannot be avoided in pursuing the journey of life.

Simply to be a member of a family is, inevitably, to enter a state in which sorrow cannot be eluded and into which separation must sooner or later come. Illness, tragedy, and death are as much a part of the "surrounding atmosphere" of the family as are oxygen, nitrogen, and carbon dioxide. We cannot by any means whatever forstall or escape them; we can at best seize hold of the kind of faith that is not shaken by any disaster.

In the end, the appropriation of such faith is one of the basic goals of the Christian family. Like all the other goals of the Christian family, this one requires deliberate striving. It is not gained easily or casually. Diligence, self-surrender, faith, and conscious effort to move toward God and His Kingdom over long periods of time are some of the spiritual essentials that must be blended and used if the latent Biblical image of the family is to be developed and made permanent.